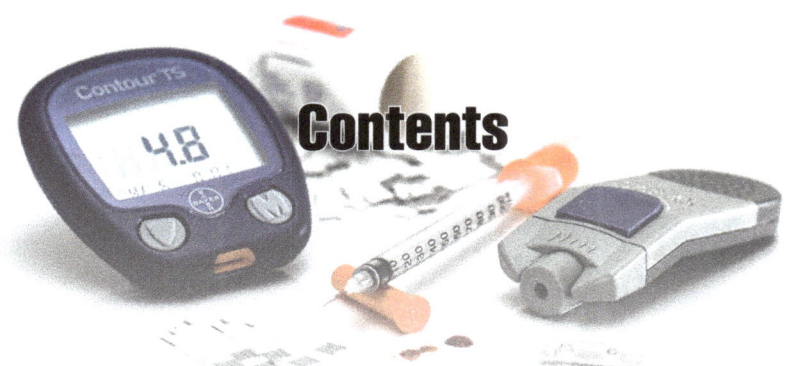

Contents

Acknowledgments 5
Diagnosis: Diabetes 7
Blisters Under My Foot 11
Hospital Visits and Surgeries 18
Depression 23
Balancing on One Foot 26
Positive Thinking, Faith, and God 29
Support Systems 32
A1C, Diet, and Exercise 39
Insulin Pump 42
Daily Rituals 45
Moving Ahead 49
Major Setback or Minor Setback? 52
"On the Bus" 55
The "New Normal" 58

T1D

Type 1 Diabetes
A Forty-Year Journey

*Jerry,
To a new friend
peace, love & happiness
♡ Cath*

Cathleen Seifert Kownacki

ISBN 978-1-64416-244-6 (paperback)
ISBN 978-1-64416-245-3 (digital)

Copyright © 2018 by Cathleen Seifert Kownacki

All rights reserved. No part of this publication may be reproduced, distributed, or transmitted in any form or by any means, including photocopying, recording, or other electronic or mechanical methods without the prior written permission of the publisher. For permission requests, solicit the publisher via the address below.

Christian Faith Publishing, Inc.
832 Park Avenue
Meadville, PA 16335
www.christianfaithpublishing.com

Printed in the United States of America

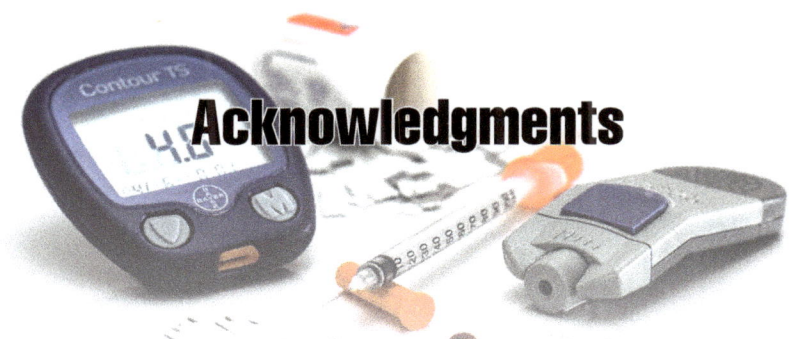

Acknowledgments

To my loving husband, Joe, who has been with me for twenty-six years and stays voluntarily through all the trials and tribulations of diabetes; and my daughter, Trisha, who was born into my diabetes thirty-six years ago. I applaud you both for your help and support; and my mom, who is the most giving and loving person I know.

Also, this book was written for all of those Type 1 diabetics who need faith and acknowledgment of their disease. It is for the parents who have a child newly diagnosed with this terrible lifelong journey.

I hope this story will give you hope and some sort of peace as I am living proof of a sustainable life after forty years.

It takes a team though with many ideas and support people as you will see in my story.

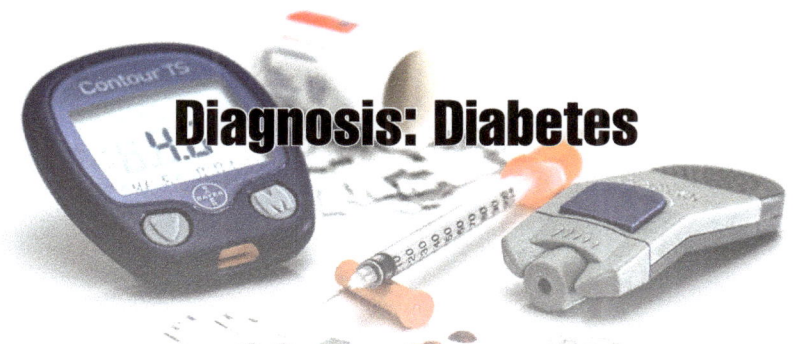

Diagnosis: Diabetes

Wow, I don't know where to start. I guess I'll start in the beginning of my journey. I used to pee in a cup and put a stick in it to see what my glucose was. Now I stick my finger four times a day with a lancet, and hopefully they can come up with something that doesn't hurt as much. But that is the least of my pain compared to what has just happened in the last three months.

It was the vascular surgeon that decided to take my foot and leg up to my knee because of the osteomyelitis infection in the bone. And the fact that the bones in the foot were deteriorating, they said, might as well start over. March 15 of 2017, I was officially an amputee. It is now three months later, and I am trying to walk with a prosthetic leg but having some problems.

I am mostly an upbeat and positive person, but I am having some real crying spells (which they said I would have) because losing a limb is like losing a part of your family. The therapist said it would take up to a year to get to the new normal, if ever—depends upon the person, I guess.

Anyway, I want to tell you of the long journey that has brought me to *now* from that person peeing in the cup forty years ago. Yes, forty years. From May 23, 1977, when I was about to graduate from community college where I was studying commercial art. I was also waitressing at national motor inn after school where Betsy and I drove from Ankeny back to Des Moines while I was changing my clothes into my uniform. By the way, those were the ugliest uniforms that I had ever seen.

I was a typical college student doing some drinking and partying, and even did my share of smoking pot. Back then in the seventies, it wasn't as bad as it is now. All of this with somewhat hard schedule could have contributed to the new diagnosis of diabetes, I don't know. All I do know was that I was nineteen and had a major disease. I didn't want anyone to know. I didn't check my pee for ketones or anything. It wasn't for a few more years that you could stick your finger to see what your blood sugar was, and I didn't want to do that either. Basically, I did not take care of myself!

I enjoyed anything that had to do with art and being creative—color theory and design were my best talents—and the logo of my initials won the praise of my teachers and the class. I loved the photography part, and used to set up the darkroom, and would spend hours in there alone processing my work. After I started the second year, things got harder and more stressful, but I was young and invincible.

I started being very thirsty and not able to drive out to school without a big glass of ice water and drinking the whole glass and eating the ice cubes before I got out there. Then I would run into the building as fast as I could to pee. I found myself peeing twelve times a day as well as losing fourteen pounds in two weeks and being so wiped out tired. My girlfriend, Nancy, at work told me she thought it sounded like diabetes, and I said, "No way." Also, the mother of my sister's boyfriend was a head nurse at one of the local hospitals, and she said diabetes also.

I was in a car accident and cracked the windshield with the side of my head (back then it wasn't required to wear seat belts like now), and you can't tell me that it didn't have something to do with the diagnosis also!

Well, it got to the point that it was my turn to drive Betsy and I to school. My dad had to drive us because I couldn't see well enough to drive. He said diabetes also. I said, "No way." They made an appointment to see the doctor, so when I got the diagnosis from him, I wasn't surprised because I had already done my crying.

Diabetes is an autoimmune disease and needs diet restriction, exercise, and insulin to control it.

From then on, I started taking insulin shots. That first one was a zinger. My mom came into the room with the needle pointing upward and stuck me in my butt, and I mean, she stuck me *hard*. I said, "From now on, I am giving myself my own shot!"

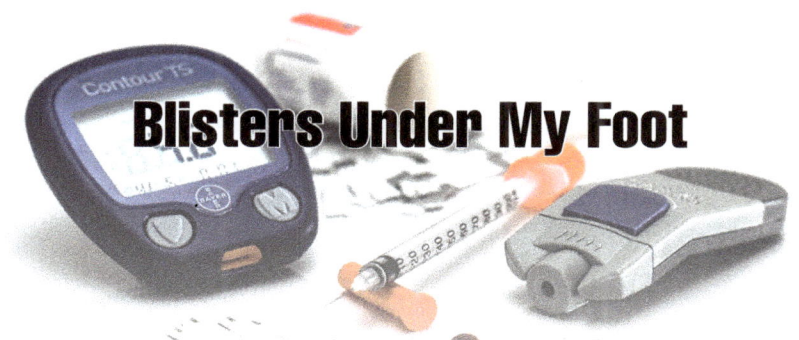

Blisters Under My Foot

Getting back to this last terrible year, it all started with a day at the pool with my youngest granddaughter, Brianna, in July 2016. I wasn't wearing pool shoes, and the heat was extremely high—ninety-five degrees. She yelled at me to get on the grass three times because she knew that I couldn't feel my feet due to neuropathy that I already had for twenty or so years. I didn't listen, and I ended up with three huge blisters on the bottom of my left foot. Well, I tried to doctor them myself and the middle one got infected to the point that it put me in the hospital.

Next thing to happen was the amputation of my middle toe and metatarsal (the small bone going down the underside of the foot). *That* was the start of the commotion of the last year. I stayed in the hospital a total of three weeks that time and was sent home with a midline (ten inches instead of a PICC line which is twenty inches). Both lines take quite a procedure, in that they raise the bed up high and put a paper sheet over me. They then put a line that started under my arm and went in the vein to the heart. They are able to put antibiotics in to you rather than an IV into my veins as I gave *no* veins left after forty years, with which to get blood in or out from this terrible disease!

The midline stays in you and mine stayed in for over a month. One nurse said I could not leave the hospital with it, and I said, "It stays, period!" It actually had to be redone three times because it clotted inside, and the antibiotics all came out back on my shirt. This is where we (my wonderful husband and I) were driving back downtown for over a month at two-thirty every day to receive my half-hour dose of antibiotics in my midline. We had to go to the hospital even on Saturday and Sunday, when that part of the hospital was shut down and got a wheelchair for me to sit on and come the long way around, what a pain!

At that point, I was in a wheelchair because now my right foot that had Charcot disease (total arch collapse) and the bones were deteriorating. I had been wearing an AFO (ankle foot orthotic) which I had put red, white, and blue stickers. If you have to wear it, it might as well be fun, right? One kind of funny note: My sister Charleen is called "Char" for short, and my sister Colleen is "Co." So when I heard Charcot (the *T* is silent), I thought how inevitable that disease is what I have—named after my two good sisters!

I have to tell you about the AFO though. To get the plastic mold off my poor foot, they had to cast it first, and I had never been casted before. It wasn't bad until they take it off with a saw—yes, a saw going up the front of my leg. Okay, I wore the first one for about two years until my right foot turned too badly, and then they made a second one. The first one had butterflies on it and always was a fun-talking point with strangers!

Like I said before, I was in sales for about fourteen years after doing desk work for about twenty; and waitressing, and other stuff for about ten, and was on my feet for most of the time I was at work. I always had good shoes on and moved fast to help the customers. I don't think the work on my feet had anything to do with my foot problems, but I think the diabetes did. After that, I am medically retired and sometimes I feel guilty, but if you saw everything I have to do to get ready every day you would understand.

My mental state is not all that great anymore either. When I was in rehab at Younker, in Methodist hospital, they noticed that they would show me something, and I would not retain it until next day when they saw me again.

One time, my husband, Joe, brought in the mail and I processed it. Writing checks, and tossing the junk, and filing the rest. Then about fifteen minutes later, I said, "When are you going to bring in the mail?" He just looked at me funny and said, "You already did the mail." Anyway, they said in rehab that it could be the trauma of the operation or just an aging thing.

Speaking of rehab, it was different from the six hospital stays I had before the operation that took my foot and partial leg due to the infection. The second one after my toe removal was two weeks in a wheelchair, and I lay around and watched TV. They brought me my tray breakfast, lunch, and dinner, but somehow I lost weight.

Then I was moved to the second place, which was a care facility for rehab on the first floor and residence downstairs. What a terrible place and experience, but again, I used the wheelchair, and they brought me my breakfast, lunch, and dinner as I lay in bed. They were understaffed and there were twenty patients for every nurse, bad.

The next place was Methodist hospital downtown, where I had the operation. It was the same thing: lying in bed and watching TV. They again brought me my meals. When I got to Younker Rehab, I was in heaven. I had gotten moved late one night to the floor. The first day I was there, the nurse came and said, "Let's get dressed." I said, "Okay," and waited. She repeated the request as I had not moved. I had been used to the nurses getting my clothes and dressing me. At Younker Rehab, it worked a bit differently. She told me to get my clothes out of the cabinet and get dressed. I transferred myself into the wheelchair next to the bed and got my clothes.

By this time, it was time for breakfast, and she said, "We eat in the dining room." *What, no breakfast in bed? Don't they know I just had my leg cut off?* This place is going to be tough. I wheeled myself down the hall to the dining room that is reserved for people on the rehab floor. Being the talkative person I am, I was thrilled to enjoy my meals in the dining room. Visiting with the other patients was great!

The food was fantastic, and I looked forward to each meal with delight. Especially great were the supreme omelets. They were *huge*, and I got in the habit of asking for only a half of omelet because a regular would fill your plate. Also great were the supreme pizzas, as well as many other items you could pick off from the menu. Believe it or not, I actually lost weight when I was there my two weeks.

Next was physical therapy (PT), occupational therapy (OT), and recreational therapy (RT). I was in heaven. There was a big gym with a fake oak tree in the middle of the room. It had a track around it with ten feet marked off and all kinds of equipment. I had always liked gym class in high school where I seemed to be the only girl who didn't mind getting sweaty (of course, that was early in the 1970s).

My schedule was like nothing I had experienced in the last four weeks. After breakfast at eight, I had PT for half hour, then OT for half hour. PT was lower body, and OT was upper body. Therapy included tasks such as emptying a dishwasher or washing machine, making easy meals, and completing other basic daily tasks. Each day I would have PT and OT again. I never had such strong arms in my life. We did leg work and eventually walked with a walker only a bit to *save* my left foot or leg from further damage, for when I got my new right leg. After therapy was lunch time, and after that was PM therapy—and the routine started again the beginning of the next day.

I made some good acquaintances while I was there and have wondered how each one of them is getting along now. I should have gotten their names and numbers but didn't think of it at that time. It kind of went fast—as fast as this last year has gone.

Do you realize it has been over a year since I have driven a car? I found out that it is about $2,500 to change over a car to hand gas and break systems. I really miss driving and going out to lunch with all of my girlfriends. I used to do all the grocery shopping, and I also miss going to walk in mall.

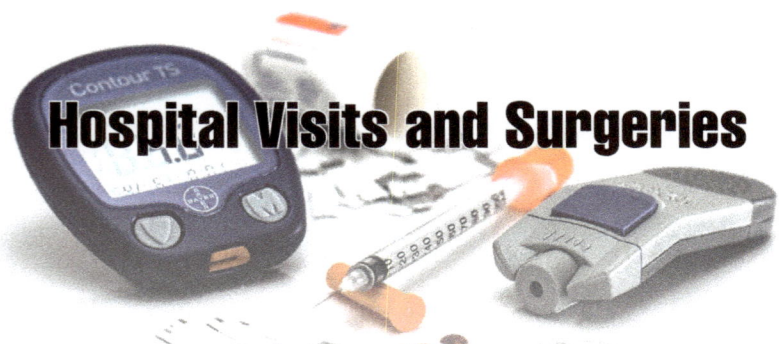

Hospital Visits and Surgeries

I had RT (recreational therapy) where we talked about depression, played cards, and I learned some new games too. After the first day, I was still in some pain and on hydrocodone, but I called my mom and told her, "I almost had fun that day eating and talking with the other patients and working out." Hence, the word *almost*. Speaking about the pain, it was the *worst* pain that I have ever had.

I have had many hospital stays in the last forty years. Some were high blood sugars like seven hundred to nine hundred, but (eighty to one hundred twenty are normal) that occurred three to four times a year that I could not get to control myself.

When I was pregnant in 1981, with my only child, Trisha, I was in the hospital in December and out for Christmas and in January 8. I had a C-section on March 23, and got out on April Fool's Day. I couldn't keep my blood sugars under control, and I didn't want to hurt (dehydrate) the baby so they hospitalized me for the whole time. Walking eighteen times around the front desk was a mile!

Another time, I walked into an outpatient clinic and said, "I think I need some antibiotics." The doctor took my blood sugar and after 6:00, it doesn't register. So the doctor did a different way to take it and came back in the room with a funny look on her face, and said my blood sugar was over nine hundred. She was in shock that I was still conscious and coherent. I said I needed to get some antibiotics that afternoon and get going because I had appointments to get to, and she said, "You are not going anywhere except the hospital and you can go by ambulance or have someone take you!" Okay, I guess I will call my husband. I forget how long I was in the hospital that time.

What people don't understand is that we, diabetics, when our blood sugar gets high we sometimes vomit and usually get dehydrated which makes it almost impossible to get an IV going. One time, it took over two and a half hours to get one going. A young man tried three times, then another person tried then another and another. Finally, a life-flight person came in and put a glove filled with hot water on my inner arms and tops of my hands, and then was able to get the IV in. Nowadays, they don't try that many times before they call Life Flight (Helicopter people). Now, I immediately ask for a *butterfly* because it looks like it has wings, or some call it a baby needle.

My friend Sylvia came and sat with me another time when I called her crying, and that I was at the hospital and that they weren't getting the IV in. I remember saying, "Maybe I should just go home." And they said, "You are already here so why don't you just stay!"

God knows how many times I have been stuck with needles. When I had my daughter, Trisha, it was so terrible, a needle in my arm four times per day and sometimes more. Later, when they tried to get blood from the top of my hand, I flat out and told them, "No." It hurt too much.

At that time, they did not have the finger sticks like they do now. I tell people that I have had one thousand blood draws out of my inner arms and hands. My veins refuse to give blood anymore. I had a very nice nurse supervisor; he helped me get one of the IV's started at one of the recent hospital stays, and he looked for a vein for over fifteen minutes before he put one in *first* try!

But all I went through having Trisha, my daughter, back in 1981, was so worth it. She has been such a joy in my life (most of the time anyway)! We are very good friends now, and I am so thankful for her.

As you know, diabetes can also be harmful to the eyes. I had the retinopathy about thirteen years ago, where they take a lazar and zap the ends of the capillaries in the back of the retina, so it does not flood the eye and make you blind like in the olden days before lasers. The doctor did about seven hundred zaps in my right eye and about one thousand two hundred in my left eye at a different time, of course. I saw what looked like a bunch of grapes in my vision; and I asked what that was, and he said it was where the laser burned the capillaries and it will go away in a while. They did go away and now I have pretty good vision. Bifocals are all.

Surgeries

If I were to put all of the operations that I have ever had:

- C-section in 1981
- Appendectomy in 1986
- Rotator cuff surgery (left shoulder) in 1995
- Achilles tendon in left ankle in 1997
- Retinopathy (laser eye surgery) both eyes in 2002
- Breast biopsy in 2005

- Along with four-inch rod they put in my right arch (to try to hold it up) in 2007
- A second right arch surgery in 2008
- Gallbladder removed in 2009
- Cataract left eye in 2011
- Angiogram in left leg to clear blockages in vein in 2016
- Middle toe and metatarsal removed (*left* foot) in 2016

Put all the surgeries together and multiply it by ten, it still would *not* equal the pain I had with this amputation surgery in 2017. If there were a hell on earth, I was in it. I truly do *not* believe that I could go through another surgery like that one. I would insist on being medically induced coma for a week.

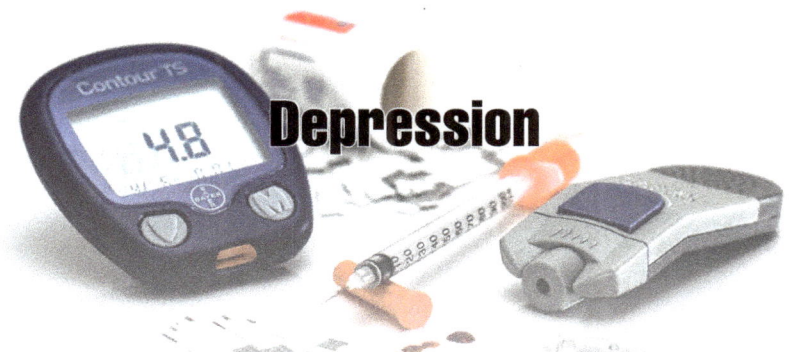

Depression

I had a complete meltdown last Saturday. It could be the depression that I think that I have always had. With writing on this story, the anniversary of the onset of the disease and the fact that I quit taking two of the three antidepressant medications cold turkey, it was the perfect storm. I couldn't quit crying. I fell out of my wheelchair and on top the floor because I did *not* have the breaks locked, and I landed on my right elbow. Years earlier, I had fallen on the ice; and I think I cracked it or pulled something out of place in there. Why I never got it checked out, I don't know. But now it huts even to type the letters (which I have a hard time with anyway).

Back to the depression. I attempted killing myself once and had my mind made up when I got in the car that morning that I was going to turn my wheel over the railing into the river. I was carrying about six hundred pounds of samples in my van and would have sank like a rock. I had a bad morning anyway. I had a big order cancel that I had worked hard on, and I got a speeding ticket. Near the time of my appointment in a nearby superb, I didn't care too much about anything. People were killing other people *just for the fun of it*, and the war kept going on overseas, and I was wondering where God was.

Thank goodness God never failed me. As I got closer to the river, there appeared a semi-truck in front of me and it caused me to move to the center lane. Then, there appeared a semi next to me on the left and one behind him. I already knew that there was an empty flatbed semi to the right of me and one behind him. I then looked in the mirror and guess what: there was a semi behind me also. I was pinned in like a baby in a baby bed, and I couldn't go anywhere! I looked over to the right, over that empty semi, and saw the river as we drove right over it. By the next exit a few miles down the road. The semis were GONE. I didn't know if they were far ahead or behind a ways but they were GONE. I was crying. If you don't believe in God or Angels—you should. (Could it have helped that I have a bead angel in both of our cars?)

I got to my destination, and I was still crying. It took a while for what just happened to sink in. I think God must have plans for me yet to come!

I met a lady while I was shopping in the mall recently. I turned a corner and she was turning the other corner and we almost ran into each other. I was in my wheelchair and she in hers. I looked at her, and I said, "You have the same leg that I have." We talked a while, and I found out she was blind and on kidney dialysis. She had a helper with her pushing her around, and I was wheeling myself.

I asked her how long she had been diabetic, and she told me, "Only five years." I said, "I had been diabetic for over forty years." We shook hands; and she went her way, and I went mine. You can have perfect blood sugars and still get complications in kidneys, eyes, limbs, and heart. It just goes to tell you we cannot control how and when—it is up to our higher power.

My counselor, Stacie, says that I am one heck of a good *fighter* and that I have been through so much. I just saw her recently and asked *why* my life so full of drama? I am glad for her and *need* someone to talk with as you would go to a medical doctor.

People always have a stigma about going to a counselor, and I tell them that it is prevention as well as necessary.

Balancing on One Foot

Try this: stand on one leg with the other one bent. Try holding on to something with one hand and try to pull your pants up. That is pretty much how it starts. Learning new balance has been one of the hardest parts about it for me. The PTs have their training on *how* to train the newly amputated patient, but the patient has to be willing, ready, and strong.

Luckily, I was strong physically to start with. When growing up, we played hard outside until dark in the summer and ate nutritiously. We (all five of us kids) were in sports and had a healthy appreciation for gym class. As a girl in the early '70s, I loved to sweat. It wasn't to cool in those days to like gym, much less participate willingly and extensively. I played basketball when it was still six-on-six–half-court. I also was on the swimming team where we swam one hundred laps per night, back and forth. I had the flattest stomach I have ever had in my life.

T1D

From there, I wanted to be a cheerleader. I had tried-out every year but not until my senior year was I chosen. You think cheerleaders just stand around and yell? Not our team. We worked on cheers and keeping all in rhythm and did unbelievable mounts that surprised everyone. I was one of the tallest (second from the end), so Colleen and I were on the bottom, and I would have one girl sitting on my shoulders and another one standing on—the one sitting on our shoulders! Maybe that's where I hurt my back.

When I was on my own, I walked a lot and did exercises at night. I had joined many health clubs with activities three nights a week. When I got married, my husband was a walker, so we would walk together. He was a faster walker than I was.

Exercise *is* so important with the diabetes, that it can actually (like I said before) with diet and weight loss, can reverse type 2 diabetes.

People always get type 1 and type 2 mixed up. I had one lady ask me, "Do you have the *bad* kind?"

"Well, both are bad," I told her. "But, yes, I take five shots of insulin in my stomach every day" (that was before I got the pump).

When I first got the diagnosis of type 1 diabetes (T1D), which some call juvenile diabetes, I was nineteen. I hear that usually juvenile diabetes means you get it when you are younger. Type 1 is different than type 2 because in type 1 people, the pancreases is *not* producing any insulin. In type 2 people, they are producing insulin *and* could get rid of their disease *if* they changed their diet, exercise, and lost weight. I would have loved that chance, but alas, we deal with the cards we are dealt. It is in our minds that we decide if we are going to rise up to the situation or face defeat.

Positive Thinking, Faith, and God

Thank goodness my faith is strong. I don't think I could have gotten through everything that I have gone through if it weren't for my faith in God. I believe that there is a supreme being that made the earth and the universe *and* has saved me from destruction many times.

That one time with the semidrivers on the bridge that saved me (who would have thought semidrivers as angels)? But there was another time too when I was younger. Like I said, I was young and didn't want anyone to *know* that I had a disease. I was drinking with the best of them and had no idea what my blood sugar was *ever*, and we were in a car. I was depressed about things, and I was in the back seat.

We were driving on Martin Luther King Parkway by the big cemetery and going around a curve. I opened my back door after I wrapped a long electric cord around my neck and jumped out. We were going only about twenty-five miles per hour and *why* I didn't die that time has always been a big question. But the only thing again was that God had more for me to do on this earth. I was nineteen.

Back to now, I haven't been to Mass since last July, and I miss it. I read my Bible weekly (I know it should be daily); but between the doctor appointments (which two are sometimes in the same day) and the PT and the daily rituals, all of a sudden it is past bedtime.

I have taken many Bible classes and know the Bible pretty well. We Catholics have many saints, and their whole life was given up to God and helping people. I want to be like them in that I have a strong need to help people.

When I had two legs, I volunteered at many places. I was a fake patient at Methodist hospital where the sets of nursing or doctor students came in, and we played a certain part that they had to deal with (this was the one that I liked the best because I have had so much practice at the real thing!).

I also put flowers together for the gift shop, and I moved wheelchairs at Fountain West to Mass every other week. Now I am one of those wheelchairs!

I think giving back to people in this world is so important. Just think how good it could be if everyone did it! I should have done more!

Next, I want to tell you of my positive attitude. Anyone can look at the glass half empty, but why not *choose* to see the glass half full? I haven't always been this positive, but I now *know* that it's the best and only way to be.

Authors note: The reason this is chapter 7 is because there are so many 7s in the Bible, especially in the last chapter (Revelation).

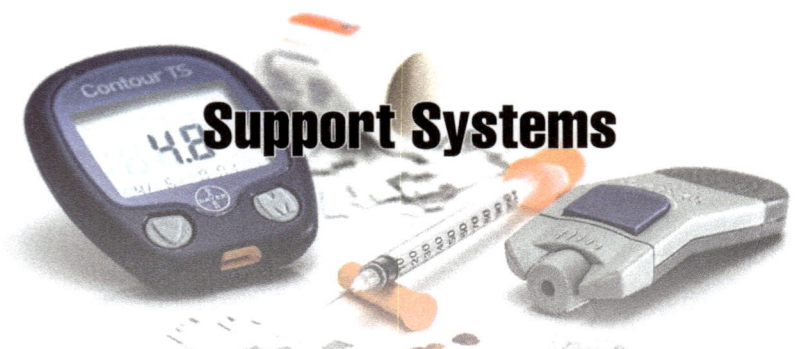

Support Systems

Everyone needs a support system, and I am fortunate to have many people in my life who give me support and courage or at least an open ear.

First, I need to tell you about my mom. *She* has been the greatest support in the last forty years. When I was first diagnosed, she turned health nut. She read and researched and learned. She would be what you would call a holistic person of today, but only back then, she learned about brewer's yeast and chromium and cinnamon. I told the doctors about these, and they laughed at me and said I was wasting my money. (Isn't it funny how these things are suggested for diabetics today?)

My mom, Elaine, read prevention magazine and went to the library because in 1977, there were no computers like today. She has helped me work through things and has been the greatest listener of my life so far. She is still learning today. I even think she may know more than the doctors. I call her with a problem and get a good answer, and then you would be surprised how many times I get the same answer from the doctors.

Just recently, I called her crying about something (and actually I call her every few days). I would say that I am pretty strong, and I have gotten it from her. She says anyone can crawl up into a hole, or they can face it head on. And I *chose* to live life to the fullest and just plain choose life and maybe help another person along the way.

We just lost my dad a few years back, and I wonder what he would have thought about my *new* leg and how I am handling things. He was a salesman who then owned his own company. My mom says, she learned her positive attitude from him.

They gave me a good upbringing with love and support. My mom is now eighty-two.

Everyone needs a support system. In addition to my amazing mother, I also have the support of my husband, Joe. I wonder if he would have married me if he had known what he was getting himself into.

I remember saying to him, "You were in boot camp, right?" He told me he was in the navy years ago. I told him having type 1 diabetes is like being in boot camp in that you always have someone riding your back. I explained that night and day every day. You can't get away from it for graduation, promotion, or even a vacation. I wasn't sure he understood what I meant at the time, but now twenty-six years later, he understands.

He lets me be in charge of taking care of myself but is always there to help when I need him. I think that with diabetes, the diabetic *has* to be in charge to *do* things for themselves as they *need* to be done.

He had gotten the whole house ready for me to come home from the last hospital and readied it for my wheelchair. He put in the ramps in the garage so that the car could still straddle the ramp and fit in the garage. He also put one on the front door step and one on the patio step.

Also, I got my walk-in tub that I had wanted for about ten years, but I guess I had to get my leg cut off to get one. Ha-ha!

There was a time I went into the hospital with a blood sugar level of over seven hundred. I was dehydrated, and they were going to put an IV in the top of my hand. I was crying as she tapped my hand hard to try and get the veins to stand up. I looked up at my husband with tears in my eyes, and he came over to me and put his hand on my shoulder.

I know with the amputation surgery he felt helpless, and his daughter said, she had never seen him cry before. He just didn't know what to do.

He doesn't say much sentimental stuff, but I know he loves me, or why would he bring me shrimp, strawberries, and flowers (to plant)?

Some of my other support people are my grown-up children and stepchildren: Trisha, Angie, Amy, and Tony. They have all helped us out doing yard work or whatever we ask of them. Trisha has taken me to my PT appointments lately to give Joe a break.

You see, to get me in the van from the house, he needs to roll me down the ramp backwards before I get myself in the car on one leg. Then to get back in the house, he pushes me up the ramp and I am not a light weight. I do believe that I am soon going to be ready to use the walker going up and down the three steps, but only if he or my son-in-law, Dusty, build me railings to hold on to. Then it wouldn't break Joe's back every time we go to doctor appointments or PT.

My two sisters, Charleen and Colleen, have also been two of my greatest supporters. I think I heard from them every day, if not every other day, and were essential for getting me through the long hospital days. Charleen is one for get well cards, and I think I got one every week from her.

My grandchildren, Destiny, Brianna, Abby, Anthony, Amanda, and Daren have all touched my life and helped in so many ways by doing things for us, and also for saying things that have helped so much. I will remember them fondly forever.

Over the years, I have made many friends, and right now I hear from them a lot. Nancy, from Ohio, is probably my longest known friend. She was the waitress who recognized my symptoms to be diabetes. She is so very smart and went on to get a master's degree.

Then there is Sylvia, whom I worked with at J. C. Penney for twelve years and who prays for me every day as I pray for her. She is eighty-three and is having some health issues herself but is solid as a rock.

My friend Vonnie was a teacher and still does some volunteer tutoring. I met her at a Bible class, and we have been good friends ever since. She comes over and brings ready-made salads so we can eat healthy. I think teachers are good ones to listen and can be a sounding board for many thoughts of life.

Dian (with no *e*) was also one whom I met at a class. It was so cool when she called and said she wanted to be *my* friend. We have a lot in common, and she *totally* understands me even as much as my mother and husband do!

My friend Sandy I had known for about twenty-three years, and I said I need to get a birthday card off to my mom as her birthday was coming up soon. She said, "Oh, when is your mom's birthday?" I told her it was June 3, and she told me that was her birthday also. It turns out she was born the same day and year as my mom! We have been great friends ever since. Her daughter, Linda, is special to me also.

There are my physical therapists Dana and Cheryl, who taught me how to live again. I learned how to hop on one foot, swivel, transfer, and rest.

There are many nurses, doctors, and therapists along the way. There were Mary Jo and Paula at Younker rehab, and Mindy and Mark at the prosthetic place, and Shelley at the HyVee Pharmacy. There is Carolyn, the diabetic doctor (who wears an insulin pump also); Lew, our financial guy; and Mike, who is my hearing aid doctor—all of whom are good friends and very good people. I have to mention Father Luis and Reverend Ed at my church as good friends and advisors also. Leighann, Jessica, and Mary were critical in helping me through Methodist North, fourth floor. There are so many people who have touched my life that I cannot remember them all. To all of them, I send my heartfelt thank you!

One more group of people I need to mention as giving me major support is Joe's relatives back east: Camille and Ron, Toni and Jerry, Theresa and Mike,

Mary, Larry and Michelle, Ronny and Patti, and cousin Barb and her husband. To each of these, a sincere thanks for the cards, calls, and flowers, and mostly the good thoughts and prayers.

A1C, Diet, and Exercise

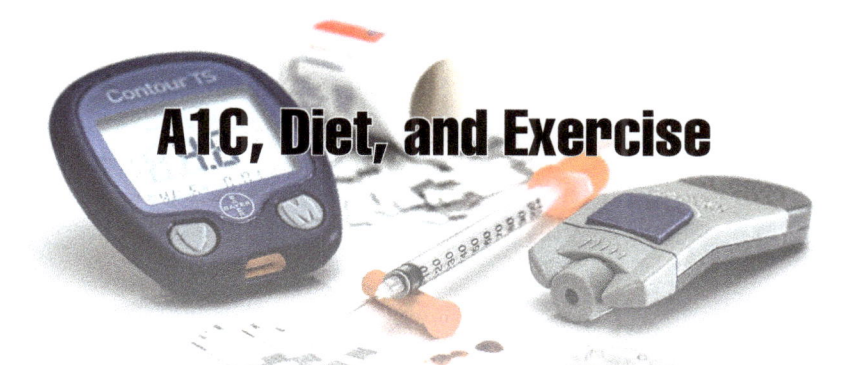

A1C is the measure of how your diabetes is doing over a three-month period. It is a test taken by the stick of the finger or by blood draw from the arm or top of the hand and produces a number hopefully around six which would be a non-diabetic number.

Mine was 11 when I was first diagnosed and now it ranges from 5.7 to 6.5. It is exciting when it goes down and that means my blood sugars are well controlled.

To control blood sugars, I need to eat more proteins and vegetables and less carbs (carbohydrates). That means limit bread groups such as pasta, breads, and things like pizza. I have to take about eight units extra of insulin to cover pizza.

Also, exercise is important. You can eat a little more if you work it off! My exercise used to consist of about a half hour of cardio (bike) and then machines. Now that I am an amputee, I haven't figured out what my workout is yet, and I really *need* to get back into it!

My blood sugar was high, 238 this morning because I was very stressed out last night and couldn't sleep. Whenever I get sick or stressed, my blood sugar goes way up, and I have to take extra insulin, drink a lot of water, and not eat anything until I test again.

Sometimes the BS (blood sugar) comes down slow and sometimes it comes down fast in which I may need to eat something sooner. It seems like a great big guessing game sometimes when you try hard but just can't get it right.

Some of my favorite foods like yogurt have different carbs for different flavors:

Vanilla: 12 carbs
Blueberry: 13 carbs
Strawberry: 14 carbs

A half bagel with butter has thirteen carbs, but if you put a small amount of jelly on it, you have to count that also (so I use sugar-free jelly and you don't have to count it). It is tricky counting my carbs and getting one unit of insulin for seven carbs (each person has different number of units of insulin per number of carbs determined by the nationalist). This part of it has always been a problem for me!

Then, when I exercise, I need to eat extra carbs and protein to keep from going to low (hypoglycemia). That can be scary as low BS can be fatal. I have never passed out from low BS but have come close. I was at twenty-eight and made my way to the kitchen bouncing off the hallway walls to get glucose tablets when I had some right next to the bed. My mind was fuzzy and my legs wobbly, and it was very scary.

Some people go the hospital when they get high or low BS. I can usually take care of it at home. Now after forty years of practice, there have been many times when I was younger that I could *not* fix myself and needed medical care.

The financial aspect of diabetes is unbelievable though, and we need to focus more on prevention with diet and exercise, especially in young overweight children who are the future.

Insulin Pump

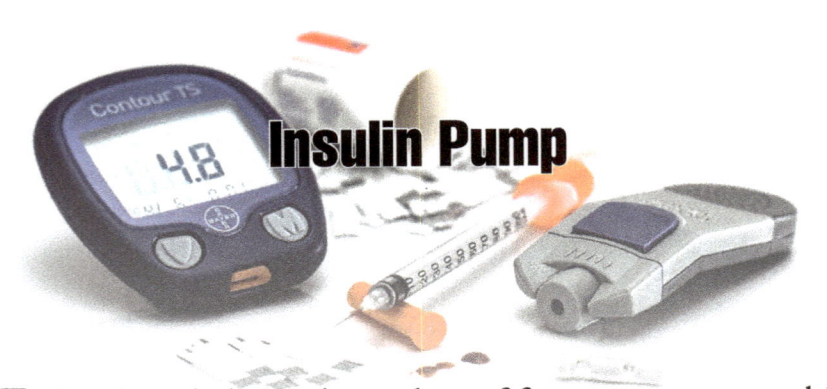

I first heard about them about fifteen years ago, and I said no. I can't do all the steps, so I just kept giving myself five shots a day in my stomach. Now that I have the pump, it is a God send. I can set it to put in insulin automatically at certain times (five times in twenty-four hour period) that is called basal rate. Also, there is bolus which means that I can add insulin when I am eating meals. The doctor always said, "Cover what you eat".

It took quite a process to get the pump. I had to prove that I was totally insulin dependent and that my body was not producing *any* insulin. There were about eight classes on how to fill the *reservoir* (the little tube inside the pump that the insulin is in) and change all the tubing and learn how to inject the small needle into my stomach. But if you think of it, I was taking five or more shots per day and now I just change the equipment every other day saving ten shots! By the way, I received my pump one day before Christmas of 2014.

It is surprising how many nurses do *not* know anything about the pump. Right after my amputation when I was on the Dilaudid pain medication (and pushing the button like Morris code) because of the great pain, I had to change the reservoir tube and they could not help me, and I was so messed up that I could not do it myself. Anyway, it seems that there needs to be more training for nurses on the pump now that more people are using it.

In the beginning, insulin was made from cows and pigs when I first started taking insulin shots back in 1977. Now it is synthetically made, and there are brands like Lantus and Novolog. One lasts for twelve hours, and the other has a twenty-four-hour time release. Tresiba is the most recent new insulin and can be used by type 1s or 2s. It also comes in pen form instead of using needles.

Who knows what will happen in the future. They already have pancreas transplants and I need to get going on getting on the transplant list where they can do a kidney or pancreas transplant at the same time. There are about three hundred people on the kidney transplant list in central Iowa, but only a few people need both. You have to qualify so they aren't just wasting resources.

You meet with a nurse, a nurse practitioner, and a counselor; you have to have a body mass index below twenty-five and have to be able to take the antirejection medication every day for the rest of your life. It is quite a process to be conserved a candidate to be put on the transplant list.

There is, of course, a cure, which they are working on right now and hopefully a cure in my lifetime.

Daily Rituals

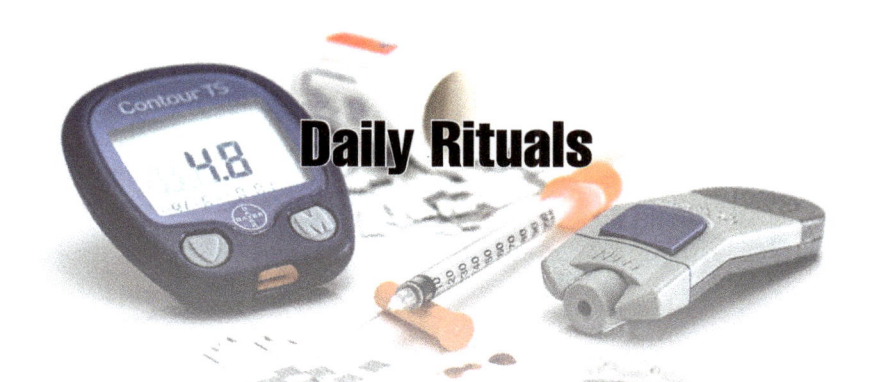

Every day there are so many things I have to do, I kind of put them in order here.

I first take off my BiPAP mask for sleep apnea and turn off the machine which I clean daily with soapy *hot* water.

After the bathroom, I return to my bedroom to put in my hearing aids which I also clean daily. If the batteries are dead, I put in new batteries and then put the red one in my right ear and the blue in my left. The batteries last about one week. I take off my foot brace on my left foot so as to protect *it* from the same fate as my right foot because the Charcot disease *could* very easily happen to that foot too!

I then go to the kitchen to test my blood sugar, so I stick my finger, put the blood drop on the stripe, and record the readings in my notebook that I keep for my doctors and myself. If they are high, I give myself some extra insulin from the insulin pump that is attached to my stomach. This alleviates four to six shots that I used to give myself every day in my stomach.

The insulin pump cartridge needs replacing along with the site in my belly every other day which takes approximately ten to fifteen minutes as there are quite a list of steps to accomplish before it is complete. However, it is not a "set it and forget it" device. It does regulate the flow of insulin more evenly as needed as opposed to shots. It is a high-tech electronic instrument with numerous programming settings and mini screens. Anytime, day or night, it gives out different warnings or alarms with various beeps or sounds that signal attention is needed. The pump is connected 24-7.

Next, I take my morning meds of nine prescriptions and some supplements. Also, in the evening, I take eight scripts and some supplements. I fill my pill box for two weeks at a time so I can have them ready for each day. This takes about twenty minutes to do. Since my eyes are getting bad, I use a magnifying glass plus my glasses to insure pills are going into their proper spots.

Breakfast usually consists of half banana, cereal, half bagel or small waffle (not too many carbohydrates as this would increase morning blood sugar). I then get dressed sitting on the edge of the bed because my balance is not very good anymore. I bath and shower using a chair next to the tub after I remove the insulin pump, of course. Afterward, I have to reconnect the pump and make sure it is working properly.

I may put some laundry in as my washer and dryer are on the ranch level of our house. I also may use the dishwasher and clean up in the kitchen. I can't do stairs anymore; I use the elevators when outside the home and right now I am still in my wheelchair. I haven't been in our basement for a very long time and never do go down there (so my husband has a "man cave" all to himself!).

With the high heat and humidity, it is hard for me to breath in the summer time. I get bent over and really struggle to breath. I get very dizzy and many times feel like I am going to pass out when outdoors. I can't do any yard work (thank goodness I have my husband). If we go anywhere, someone has to lift the wheelchair out of the back of the van and it is quite a chore.

I can put dishes away in the cupboards from the dishwasher, but I have my two teenage granddaughters do some vacuuming and general cleaning when they are here. They may also do some cooking (if not, we just eat simply).

During the day, I watch some TV and check e-mails and answer correspondence. I can't sit very long, and I can't stand without the walker so I try to move around in the house occasionally during the day.

Around 11:00 a.m., it is time to check my blood sugars again, then at 3:00 and 7:00 p.m. unless my sugars are high. Then it is every hour. Type 1 diabetes is a time-consuming disease and takes constant planning of insulin coverage and food to manage it. Sometimes it is just a guessing game.

Around 6:00 p.m., I take my night pills (again some scripts and some supplements). Supper may consist of a salad or a sandwich or a frozen pizza with some veggies and fruit. We try to eat four to five servings of fruits and veggies per day. I even fried hamburger on the stove the other day! *And* I can get things on and out of the microwave (carefully not to dump it on my head) and work up a good meal.

At bedtime, I take off my rubber sock, wash it with soap and water, and spray it with an alcohol-water mix and hang it on its hanger. I put the pink Post-it note on the second sock for the next day. I take out my hearing aids and put on my BiPAP mask. I take pain meds as needed, and if it gets to be 11:00 p.m., I may take half of a sleeping pill.

I am glad to sleep at night, but I am even *gladder* to wake up the next day.

Moving Ahead

Back to now. We have been in contact with the surgeon to see if he can shave the front bone that is causing me trouble on the front of my leg so my prosthetic won't hurt so much. He said, "Well, we can do another surgery to take off another inch." And I replied, "No, thank you, it hurt too much the first time." It's always something, right?

If they can't do anything about it, I will try putting more socks on. The socks come in different plies. They look like a big flat bag with a hole in the bottom.

There is a thin (no. 1) and a medium (no. 3) and a heavy one (no. 5). The other day, I had on two (no. 3) and one (no. 5), so I had on eleven plies, and the front of that bone still hurts badly when I was walking with my *new* leg on using the walker. I even tried walking with a cane and holding Cheryl's arm (my physical therapist).

It's all been moving quite fast since March 15 (the day of the amputation). In that, the training has been quite extensive. I had to learn how to transfer from the wheelchair to the bed and back to the wheelchair. I took showers by transferring to the shower chair from the wheelchair. The big one was when I had to learn how to get into the van from the wheelchair. I was really scared of that one. But the great PTs and OTs taught me well, and I have all the respect for what those people do. Then, I had to learn to swivel using my stationery leg to move my foot back and forth so as to turn around or get somewhere (while holding onto the walker).

I have come a long way since the beginning journey of the amputation process, also in the diabetes journey. I keep a notebook of my blood-sugar tests when I stick my finger at 7:00 a.m., 11:00 a.m., 3:00 p.m., and 7:00 p.m., and I write them down. This allows me to see a pattern if I need to increase the amount of insulin.

I am not the perfect diabetic by any means, but I do try now more than ever.

We cannot know when we are young that our actions may hurt us when we are older. Like my drinking or eating lots of chocolate or sugar.

When I first became diabetic, I remember the doctor saying that I would not be able to have children, and

I wouldn't live very long. The treatments have come so very far, and the future holds even more unbelievable treatments that I can't wait to see what they come up with next.

I can tell you that I don't regret anything in my life, and I would do it all over again. My life has been full and rich with all the people I have met along the way and experiences that I will never forget!

Major Setback or Minor Setback?

This was one of those days that my BS was high—303 (without eating anything out of the ordinary last night). Well, I thought I was doing better with my prosthetic leg and using the cane, but I had a doctor's appointment with the vascular people yesterday, and my prosthetic doctor was also there since every time I put the leg on the front bone it *hurt*.

They saw a sore at the bottom of my skin at the amputation site and found there to be fluid in it. They took a sample and sent it to the lab *stat* and started me on three-a-day antibiotics for seven days. The top (front) of my bone is hot and red and swollen and now I can't wear my leg or go to PT for a month to let it heal.

Instead, I went straight to the hospital and had a PICC line (twenty inches) under my left arm. That was Thursday, July 20. They used Vancomycin, one of the strongest antibiotics (so far) to rid of the osteomyelitis

T1D

in my IV that ran for one and a half hours per day and did another MRI.

Friday, July 21. I think waiting for the test results is almost the worst part. If the osteomyelitis has come back, it would mean another surgery and I said I wouldn't have another surgery. It would mean a cut below my knee or above the knee which would be really bad.

Saturday, July 22. The infectious disease. Doctor came in and said the MRI showed infection in the bone, and they would be doing another surgery. My mind is going crazy. I don't want another surgery, but the alternative is surly death from this infection. Only one in ten thousand people get this infection (usually diabetics and people with diminished immune systems). The bacteria are present on almost everyone's skin all the time.

Sunday, July 23. Church day. "O God, where are you?" I no more than thought this, and one of my priest friends came in. He said, "God's in charge, and his healing grace will save you."

Monday, July 24. Still waiting to hear when the surgery will be but have decided to be okay with it.

Tuesday, July 25. Every day I see the vascular doctors, the surgeon, the infectious-disease people, the kidney doctor, the social worker, and the care coordinator. Most of the time, they all come separately, but sometimes they overlap.

Wednesday, July 26. Peaceful and feeling like a queen. They bring me my meals in bed. I watch TV, and they bathe me, and eighteen times around the front desk is a mile in my wheelchair. Not thinking about the surgery.

Thursday, July 27. Scared. I cried—again.

Friday, July 28. Second amputee surgery of two and a half more inches due to osteomyelitis; setback six months. I opened my Bible, and it fell to this psalm:

> Find rest, oh my soul, in God alone,
> My hope comes from Him.
> He alone is my rock and my salvation.
> He is my fortress, I shall not be shaken.
> (Psalm 62)

"On the Bus"

They asked me after the surgery did I know where I was?

I said, "On the bus." (I haven't ridden a bus in fifty years!)

They said, "No, try again."

Well, I said, "I am in a bed."

And they said, "Yes, and where are these beds?"

I said, "In a hospital?"

And they said, "Which hospital?"

I said, "Des Moines, Iowa."

"Yes," they said, "but which hospital in Des Moines."

I said, "Methodist hospital."

They must have given me more pain medicine than the first time because this is how my brain worked for about four days after the surgery. People have told me all the crazy things I had been saying, and I was really far out there. I can remember the minute I got back, and my daughter, Trisha, was crying because she didn't think I would get back.

Now that I am healing, *again*, I have twelve doctors:

- Podiatry
- Pulmonary
- Kidney
- Infectious disease
- Endocrinology
- Vascular
- Surgeon
- Pain management
- Gynecology
- Retina specialist
- Hearing aid
- And then there is the very important—Counselor.

There was a woman who came into my room one day to give me Communion. I told her I was writing a book and that I had forty years as a type 1. She asked me if I remembered any of my previous doctors, and I told her about Dr. Bassiri, my first doctor, and she said her parents were very good friends with him. Then I said, "Dr. Purtle was next but that he became a teacher after doctoring me for about six or seven years. Then he went on to be a teacher." Her eyes lit up, and she said that was her husband and that he is now very high up in the administration of the four hospitals. He was a good doctor, and I learned a lot from him.

I know that we have to accept what God lays at our feet, be happy, and go on. It is so hard sometimes, but he never gives us more than what we can handle. Although, eight hospital visits (from June of 2016 to July of 2017) in one year is a little bit much.

The "New Normal"

Wow! I have come to the end of my story for now. Not so sure what will come next. My eyes are not doing so well these days, and I am down to one kidney, but my heart is good. Not sure if I am ever going to be able to *walk* again, but I will give it a good try.

But I know that I have had a good *run* of it for forty years, and I usually landed on my "feet" or should I now say "foot." Hasn't always been a walk in the park, but I think of how many times I have crossed the *finish line*. If you consider all the things that have happened to me, I still think I have come out of it *head and heels* above the average person.

Abraham Lincoln once said, "I used to complain about not having shoes until I met a man who had no feet."

There are always folks out there that have it a lot worse than I do. With God, family, friends, and a fantastic husband on my side, I can make it through anything!

About the Author

Cathy Kownacki's mission since the forty years of type 1 diabetes journey and recent leg amputation is to never give up. We must accept the hardships of life and keep going.

She was instructed to bring a message of hope, kindness, and love of God to the world. Also, a word of thankfulness as there are those folks out there who have it a lot worse.

Cathy lives with her wonderful husband, who has really taken hold of the situation and made an extremely difficult time better by his presence and figuring out what to do.

CPSIA information can be obtained
at www.ICGtesting.com
Printed in the USA
JSHW050428300123
36871JS00008B/94

9 781644 162446